South Carolina Fish Species

Game Fish & Panfish

Billy Grinslott – Kinsey Marie Books

ISBN - 9781968228422

Orange spotted sunfish are mostly found in floodplains of the United States of the Great Lakes. Its beautiful shiny silvery-blue body has reddish-orange spots, which give it its name, orange spotted sunfish. They are most abundant in large muddy rivers, reservoirs, and streams. but are too small to be popular with anglers. Their average length is 3 inches. They are a small fish.

Redear sunfish are known for their red or orange-edged gill flaps. They are a type of sunfish that thrive in warm, quiet waters, feeding primarily on mollusks and snails, and can grow up to 12 inches and weigh as much as 2 pounds. They are also known as shellcracker, due to their diet and the way they crush shells. The redear sunfish will thrive in most warm-water lakes and streams.

Longear sunfish are small, thin-bodied fish with a unique long ear flap on their gill cover, that how they got their name long ear. They are often mistaken for a pumpkinseed. They have an olive to rusty-brown back, a bright orange belly. They typically reach a length of 4.5 inches. They are mostly active during the day and inactive at night.

Redspotted sunfish prefer slow-moving waters with abundant vegetation, such as backwaters, swamps, and lakes. Redspotted sunfish are largely insectivorous, consuming midge larvae and other aquatic insects. They are distinguished by an iridescent turquoise crescent around their eye and silvery, creamy, or white margins on their fins. The redspotted sunfish grows to a maximum standard length of 6.3 inches.

The Warmouth is a member of the Rock Bass, Green Sunfish and Bluegill family. They can survive in low oxygen environments while other fish cannot. Warmouth can thrive in muddy water, when other fish can't. Warmouth are often confused with rock bass. The difference between the two is in the anal fin: warmouth have three spines on the anal fin ray and rock bass have six spines.

Dollar sunfish are pint-sized sunfish, typically reaching 4-5 inches in length. They have a black opercular flap, the flap covering the gills, that is adorned with wavy blue lines or specks. They inhabit pools of creeks and small to medium rivers, as well as swamps and areas with cover like woody debris.

The bluegill also considered a sunfish is the most popular fish to fish for. They are called pan fish because they are about the size of a frying pan. Bluegills love to eat insects and bugs. They have good vision and rely on their keen eyesight to feed. Three types in this group are the Bluegill, Sunfish, and Pumpkinseed.

The Green Sunfish is blue green in color. It has yellow flecks on both its scales and some parts of its sides. The Green Sunfish also has broken blue stripes which is why some people confuse it with the Bluegill. Green Sunfish are very adaptable. They can live in any body of water that has vegetation or weeds. Green sunfish are opportunistic feeders, consuming insects, small fish, and other invertebrates.

The Redbreast sunfish has a red-yellow chest and belly with rusty brown spots on their body. The species is known for its distinctive grunting vocalizations, which are produced by grinding their teeth together. Redbreast sunfish can survive in oxygen-poor environments by using their gills to extract oxygen from air bubbles trapped in aquatic vegetation.

The Pumpkinseed is also known as pond perch, sun perch, and punky's sunfish. It can be found in numerous lakes, ponds, and rivers. It is their body shape resembling the seed of a pumpkin, that inspired their name. Pumpkinseed sunfish have speckles on their orangish colored sides and back, with a yellow to orange belly and chest. They are active during the day and rest at night near the bottom or in shelter areas.

The Rock Bass is not actually a bass but a member of the sunfish family. They are often called red eye or goggle eye due to their distinctive bright red eyes. The biggest Rock Bass ever caught on record weighs about three pounds and was a little over one foot long. Rock bass prefer waters with rocky vegetated areas, that's how they got their name.

The Bluebarred Pygmy Sunfish is a tiny, secretive fish, known for its stunning blue-black patterns. The Freshwater Bluebarred Pygmy Sunfish is found in South Carolina, endemic to its Coastal Plain, specifically in the Savannah, Edisto, and New River drainages, often found in vegetated creeks, sloughs, and roadside ditches, but is considered vulnerable due to habitat threats. They are tiny fish, reaching only about 1 to 3 inches in length, and are often found among dense aquatic plants.

The Flier is a small, sunfish known for its olive-green color, rows of dark spots, and a dark teardrop or streak below its eye, with large dorsal and anal fins. It inhabits slow-moving, clear waters in the Southern U.S. coastal plains and Mississippi river basin. They feed on insects, snails, worms, leeches, crustaceans, and small fish, also some phytoplankton.

Spotted sunfish are commonly found in backwater streams, coastal plain rivers, and ponds. They are known for their iridescent blue eye patch and small size. They are often called stumpknockers, because they love to hang out in and feed around submerged logs, stumps, and other woody debris. They thrive in warmer, slow-moving waters with sandy or rocky bottoms, and biting well on lures and bait.

There are two main types of crappies. The white crappie and the black crappie. They are also members of the sunfish family. The difference between the white and black crappie is one has dark spots and the other has dark lines and is lighter in color. The white crappie has six dorsal fin spines, whereas the black crappie has eight dorsal fin spines. The white crappie can grow bigger and more of the bigger white crappie are caught in North America. The biggest crappie ever caught in South Carolina was a 5-pound, 1-ounce white crappie.

The two most famous perches are the common perch and the yellow perch. The yellow perch has a brilliant greenish yellow color with orange fins. The yellow perch is the biggest one and can grow to a size of 18 inches. It's also known as the jumbo perch. The other type of perch is the white perch. The biggest yellow perch caught in South Carolina weighed 3 pounds, 4 ounces.

White perch grow seven to ten inches in length and rarely weigh more than one pound. They have a silvery body with faint lines on the sides. The white perch is an opportunistic feeder. Young feed primarily on zooplankton and adults feed on aquatic insect larvae, minnows and fish eggs. White Perch is a euryhaline species, inhabiting fresh, brackish and coastal waters. The biggest White Perch caught in South Carolina, is a tie between two fish weighing 1 pound, 15.2 ounces.

There are several types of sucker fish. The sucker fish has the same mouth as a carp. They got their name because their mouth is like a suction cup. They normally are bottom feeders and suck their food from the bottom of the lake. Many people use sucker fish as bait to fish for northern pike and other big game fish. The largest individual sucker fish recorded as a state record in South Carolina is a Notchlip Sucker weighing 12 lbs. 11 oz.

Redhorse are large, bottom-feeding freshwater sucker fish known for their reddish fins, and molar-like throat teeth that they use to crush mollusks. They inhabit in clear rivers with gravelly bottoms, where they feed on insects and detritus. They spawn in spring, often migrating upstream. They are popular with anglers for their strong fight, when catching them in swift currents. They can grow to around 18 pounds and 30 inches long,

Buffalo Fish are sometimes confused with carp. Buffalo fish have a downward-facing mouth, capable of sucking bits of food out of the silt and sand on the bottom. They have broad bodies, blunt heads, and silvery gray or brown scales. Buffalo fish are members of the suckerfish family. Buffalo fish, especially bigmouth and smallmouth varieties, can grow quite large, with reports of fish over 80 pounds and even reaching 100 years old.

Male drum fish also known as sheepshead or gaspergou. make a rumbling or grunting sound by contracting muscles along their air bladder walls. They have large, ivory-like ear bones that can be up to an inch in diameter, which Native Americans used as necklaces or bracelets and sometimes referred to as the lucky stones. Freshwater drum are primarily bottom feeders, spending much of their time near the bottom of lakes and rivers in search of food. The official state record is an 89-pound Black Drum.

Carp have long been an important food fish to humans. Carp are bottom feeders for the most part and their mouth is made like a suction cup, so they can suck food off the bottom. Carp are good for a lake because they help clean the bottom of the lake. Carp are introduced for aquatic vegetation control and can grow very large. The biggest officially recognized common carp record in South Carolina is 58 pounds.

There are few different species of Gar, the Longnose gar, Short nose and Alligator gar. The Long Nose Gar got its name because of its long mouth that looks like an alligator's mouth. The alligator gar is one of the biggest freshwater fish growing up to 10 feet long. The world record for a catch was set at 327 pounds. The biggest reported longnose gar caught in South Carolina weighed 28 pounds, 12.8 ounces.

Sturgeons have sharp spines on their back, so be careful when handling them. Instead of scales, sturgeon skin is covered in bony plates called scutes, which can be very sharp on young sturgeon. Sturgeons have been around since the dinosaur days. Sturgeons mostly live in large, freshwater lakes and rivers. Their average lifespan is 50 to 60 years. South Carolina has documented specimens over 8 feet long and 149 pounds,

The black, brown and yellow bullhead are part of the catfish family. They usually only grow to about 10 inches long. They use their whiskers to help find food. The bullhead is the most common member of the catfish family. Bullheads live in the water containing low oxygen levels. They can survive on low oxygen areas, where other fish can't. The largest bullhead catfish ever caught in South Carolina weighed 6 pounds, 6.3 ounces.

Flathead Catfish, their body is wide but flattened and very low in height. Both eyes are on the top of the flattened head, giving excellent vision to see upward. Flathead catfish live mainly in large bodies of water like big rivers and reservoirs. They prefer deep pools of water. The largest Flathead Catfish caught in South Carolina was an 84-pound, 9.6-ounce giant.

The Channel Catfish are the most fished catfish species with around 8 million anglers fishing for them per year. Channel catfish have taste buds all over their body, making them highly sensitive to the taste and smell of food. They also have barbels (whiskers) around their mouths, which are used for sensing and tasting food. They use sound waves to communicate with each other. They can also produce alarm substances to warn other catfish of danger. The largest Channel Catfish ever caught in South Carolina, weighed 58 pounds.

There are several species of catfish. Blue catfish are known for their size, reaching over 100 pounds. Blue catfish, like other catfish, lack scales and have smooth skin. They have barbels (whiskers) around their mouths, which are used for sensing and tasting food. They are generally slate blue on the back and silvery/white on the underside. The largest blue catfish caught in South Carolina, and the current state record, weighed 113.8 pounds. The massive fish measured 52 inches long with a 40-inch girth.

Bowfins can breathe both air and water, putting them at an advantage in low-oxygen waters. Bowfins are often described as prehistoric relics. This is because species can be traced to fossils from the Cretaceous, Eocene and Jurassic period. The largest bowfin caught in South Carolina weighed 21 pounds, 8 ounces.

White Bass or striped bass range in color from a silvery white to a pale green. Their backs are mostly black, while their sides and belly are pale with stripes running along them. White Bass are related to Striped Bass and called wipers. The general world record for a white bass is around 6.8 pounds.

Striped bass are often called Stripers. Striped bass live in both salt and fresh water. Striped bass have very sensitive eyes and will seek deep water when the sun is out. Striped bass have a preferred water temperature range of from 55° F to 68° F, and swim to find water of these temperatures. White Bass are related to Striped Bass and have lighter stripes on their sides. The largest striped bass caught in South Carolina and held as the state record is 63 pounds.

Alabama spotted bass are a type of black bass. They are often mistaken for a true spotted bass but are more elongated and tend to weigh less per inch. A key characteristic is a dark, blotchy lateral band from head to tail with spots below the band. Alabama spotted bass prefer clear, deep water with rocky substrates, and are less common in turbid waters or areas with sand or mud substrates. The state record for the Spotted Bass is 8-pound, 5-ounces.

Redeye Bass got their name because they have red in their eyes. Redeye bass are smaller than other black bass species, typically reaching 6-10 inches in length. They have an olive body that turns to white along the belly. They often have white and orange margins on their tail fin. Redeye bass thrive in small, clear streams with rocky bottoms. Redeye bass are known for their aggressive strong scrappy fights, making them a popular target for flyfishing anglers. The largest Redeye Bass caught in South Carolina, weighed 5 pounds, 2.5 ounces.

Smallmouth bass have a smaller mouth than the largemouth bass. They also have different markings and are lighter in color. They don't live in most lakes because they prefer living in colder water. They are typically found in the northern states in America because the water is cooler. The current world record smallmouth is an 11-pound, 15-ounce fish caught in Dale Hollow Lake. The largest officially recorded Smallmouth Bass in South Carolina weighed 9 pounds, 7 ounces.

The largemouth bass is the most sought-after bass in North America. Largemouth bass live in just about every lake in North America. They have great hearing and can hear a crayfish crawling on the bottom of the lake. The largest largemouth bass caught in South Carolina weighed 16 pounds, 2 ounces.

The sauger is part of the walleye family. There are 2 different types of saugers. The normal sauger and the suageye. The saugeye is a mix of the sauger and walleye. The suageye have white eyes just like the walleye. The sauger and suageye are smaller than the walleye. Saugers are more likely to be found in large rivers with deep pools but are also found in lakes. The all-time world record sauger weighed 8 pounds, 12 ounces.

The walleye got its name because of its white looking eyes. Their eyes collect light, even in low light conditions. This means they can see in the dark. Because they can see in the dark, they mostly feed at night. During the daytime their eyes are very sensitive, so they usually head for deeper water or shady places. Walleye like to live in cooler water and are normally found in the upper part of North America. The largest walleye caught in South Carolina weighed 10 pounds, 1.44 ounces.

Pickerel, also called pike in SC, look like northern pike, but they are not. The Pike is larger in size than the Pickerel. The Pickerel has more spots than the Pike, but the Pike has spots on its fins and pickerel don't. The Pickerel has a dark bar beneath their eyes and northern pike don't. There are 3 types of Pickerel in South Carolina, Chain Pickerel, Redfin Pickerel, and Grass Pickerel. The largest pickerel caught in South Carolina is a Chain Pickerel (Jackfish) weighing 6 pounds, 4 ounces.

The muskellunge called the Musky or Muskie for short is one of the biggest game fish in freshwater lakes. While Giant Pike aren't native or common in South Carolina, there's a small, isolated population of Giant Pike (Muskellunge) in the upper stretches of the Broad River. They're stocked and sought by anglers in these connected cool-water river systems. The largest giant pike recorded in South Carolina, according to the SCDNR website, is a Muskellunge (Muskie) weighing 22 pounds, 8 ounces.

Brook trout are characterized by their olive-green bodies with pale, worm-like markings, red spots with bluish halos, and orange-red fins with white and black edges. They can grow up to 12 inches in length. Brook trout are cold-water fish that prefer clean, clear, and cold streams, lakes, and ponds. The largest officially recognized Brook Trout in South Carolina weighed 4 pounds, 10 ounces.

Brown trout can live up to 20 years. Brown exhibits a variety of colors and spotting patterns, with red spots surrounded by blue halos and black spots being common. Brown trout have higher tolerance for warmer waters than either the brook or rainbow trout. Brown trout can be found on almost every continent except Antarctica. The largest brown trout caught in South Carolina weighed 17 pounds, 9.5 ounces.

The rainbow trout gets its name because of its brilliant colors. Rainbow trout populations are good indicators of water pollution because they can only survive in clean waters. They like to live in rivers and streams. Rainbow trout rank among the top five most sought game fish in North America. The largest rainbow trout caught in South Carolina weighed 11 pounds, 5 ounces.

Interesting Fish Facts in South Carolina.

South Carolina's official state fish, the Striped Bass, can grow large (over 40 lbs.) and lives in both freshwater and saltwater.

The massive Blue Catfish was introduced to SC in 1964 and thrives in lakes like Lake Marion.

The Robust Redhorse was rediscovered in the Oconee River in 1991 and is found in the Savannah and Pee Dee Rivers.

South Carolina is home to unique fish like the bluebarred pygmy sunfish, a species found nowhere else.

The state hosts more than nine native sunfish species, including redeye bass, bluegill, and shellcrackers.

Fish like Gar are hard to catch, requiring skill and stout tackle to catch.

Brook Trout, found in cool mountain streams, are less competitive and face high mortality rates early in life.

There are over 35,000 miles of freshwater rivers and streams in SC.

Author Page

Billy Grinslott – Kinsey Marie Books

ISBN – 9781968228422

Thanks

www.ingramcontent.com/pod-product-compliance
Lightning Source LLC
Chambersburg PA
CBHW060849270326
41934CB00002B/55